The Solar System

By Carmen Bredeson

Consultants
Dr. Orsola De Marco
Department of Astrophysics
American Museum of Natural History
New York, New York

Katy Kane
Educational Consultant

Jeanne Clidas, Ph.D.
National Literacy Consultant

Children's Press®
A Division of Scholastic Inc.
New York   Toronto   London   Auckland   Sydney
Mexico City   New Delhi   Hong Kong
Danbury, Connecticut

Designer: Herman Adler Design
Photo Researcher: Caroline Anderson
The photo on the cover shows the solar system.

Library of Congress Cataloging-in-Publication Data

Bredeson, Carmen.
  The solar system / by Carmen Bredeson.
    p. cm. — (Rookie read-about science)
  Includes index.
  Summary: An introduction to the planets of our solar system and other
  features such as asteroids, meteoroids, comets, and moons.
    ISBN 0-516-22865-X (lib. bdg.)   0-516-27771-5 (pbk.)
    1. Solar system—Juvenile literature. [1. Solar system. 2. Planets.]
  I. Title. II. Series.
  QB501.3 .B74 2003
  523.2—dc21   2002011217

JE
BRE
C.1

$14.25

Did you know that our big, bright Sun has a family? The Sun's family is called the solar system.

Planets and their moons
travel around the Sun.
So do asteroids, meteoroids,
and comets. They are all
part of the solar system.

Asteroids and meteoroids
are space rocks. Some
asteroids are as big as
a mountain.

Meteoroids are smaller
than asteroids. They can be
as small as a grain of sand.

Asteroid

A comet is like a big snowball with a rock in the middle.

Comets start to melt when they get close to the Sun. A melting comet has a long tail.

Planets are an important part of the solar system. Nine planets go around the Sun.

11

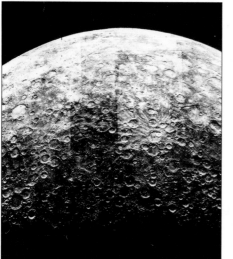

Mercury

Venus

Earth

Mars

The four planets closest
to the Sun are called rocky
planets. Mercury, Venus,
Earth, and Mars are made
of rock.

Mars is the red planet.
Iron in the soil gives Mars
a red color. Many space
probes have visited Mars.

Jupiter

Saturn

Uranus

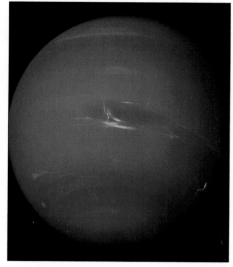

Neptune

The next four planets are called gas giants. Jupiter, Saturn, Uranus, and Neptune are made of gas.

You could not stand on them. It would be like trying to stand on a cloud.

Saturn has beautiful rings
around it. The rings are
made of pieces of ice.
Some of the pieces are
as big as a house!

The farthest known planet in the solar system is Pluto. It is smaller than Earth's moon. Pluto is solid like the rocky planets.

There are many moons in the solar system. Most of the planets have at least one moon. Only Mercury and Venus have no moons at all.

Moons of Saturn

Earth has one moon.

Jupiter has thirty-nine moons!

On Earth, we have air to breathe and water to drink. Crops grow in the warm sunshine. Earth is just right for living things.

The night sky is full of lights. Most of the lights are stars like our Sun. Some of those stars have planets.

Could there be another planet like Earth?

Words You Know

asteroid

comet

moons

planets

30

solar system

space probe

Index

About the Author

Carmen Bredeson has written dozens of nonfiction books for children. She lives in Texas and enjoys traveling and doing research for her books.

Photo Credits

Photographs © 2003: Corbis Images: 28 (Matthias Kulka), 27 (Karl Weatherley), 23, 30 bottom left; NASA/Goddard Space Flight Center: 12 bottom left; NASA/JPL/Caltech: 7, 12 top right, 12 bottom right, 16 bottom right, 16 top left, 16 top right, 16 bottom left, 19, 24, 30 top left; Photo Researchers, NY: 4, 31 top (David Hardy/SPL), 20 (Roger Harris/SPL), 12 top left, 15, 31 bottom (NASA/SPL), cover, 3, 11, 25, 30 bottom right (SPL), 8, 30 top right (Detlev van Ravenswaay/SPL).